OOPS!
IS THERE A
MOTHER
IN THE
TRINITY?

ALRIC NIYI AMON

Opps! Is There A Mother In The Trinity?
Copyright © 2005 by Alric Niyi Amon

Published by
Sophos Books Ltd.
2 Woodberry Grove
London
N12 0DR
www.publishwithsophos.com

All Scripture quotations are taken from the *King James Version*
of the Bible.

ISBN 978-1-905669-67-7

Cover design by *Icon Media*

Printed in the United States of America

CONTENTS

I dedicate this book to Eniola, my eternal sweetheart, God's gift to me… and my four children (the fruit of motherhood): Talodabioluwa (who is like the Lord), Oluwajohungbogbolo (God is greater than all things), Eninlaloluwa (the Lord is great) and Tanitoluwa (who is as great as God).

CHAPTER 1
YOU OUGHT TO KNOW

Esmeralda glanced nervously at the clock on the hospital wall for the umpteenth time. This baby is really taking its time, she thought, chewing her bottom lip unconsciously. I thought I was through when I had Irene, she mused. With a little smile forming at the corner of her lips, she caressed her bloated abdomen with obvious affection and pondered on what name to call the infant that curled snugly in her womb, already two weeks overdue.

All of a sudden, a sharp pain shattered her reverie. Her knuckles turned pale and bloodless as she gripped the side of the hospital bed. Her screams reverberated through the labor ward, as wave after wave of birth pangs surged through her. "Nurse, nurse the baby is coming, the baby is coming", she blurted out.

At quarter to midnight the healthy screams of a defiant infant filled the air. He yelled at the adults who had conspired to bring him out of the cozy enclosure of his mother's womb, into the pathos filled amphitheater of life. I had arrived... in style.

I happen to be the last of six children. My mother had decided to stop having children before I was conceived. But I guess God had other plans. I know for sure you wouldn't be reading this book if God didn't push my parents on. Aren't you grateful God has a plan? I am.

There is something about motherhood: it affects every level of humanity. Every human that walks on the face of this earth came into existence because of a woman.

When God first spoke to me about the Holy Spirit being a symbol of motherhood, I had never seen anyone stand up in a church pulpit and preach it. I never read it in any book or saw it on any video tape. From the pages of the Bible, the Spirit Himself showed me scriptural proof, that HE is the symbol of MOTHERHOOD in the

Trinity. Over and over, as I have shared this truth in various places, God has confirmed the message with His awesome presence. As I wrote a certain section of this book, a friend of mine commented... "It seems you wrote this book for women"? Well, let me respond to that statement ...This book is for both MEN and WOMEN. It's about the Holy Spirit. The Holy Spirit lives inside both MEN and WOMEN. This particular revelation about the Holy Spirit will affect not only women but also men. The Holy Spirit is NOT a woman... HE is the SYMBOL OF MOTHERHOOD in the Trinity. There is a difference between being a "woman" and being a symbol of "MOTHERHOOD". Motherhood concerns us all, how much more, the ministry of MOTHERHOOD of the Spirit of God.

In the scriptures we find the story of the Berean Jews. The Bible says they were more noble than the Jews of Thessalonica... the scriptures give the reason why.

These were more NOBLE than those in Thessalonica, in that they RECEIVED the word with all readiness of mind, and SEARCHED the scriptures daily, whether those things were so. (Acts 17:11)

This group of people not only received the word, but they took another step ... they SEARCHED the scriptures DAILY to find out, if the things they were told were TRUE! As you read through this book, I encourage you to personally look up every scripture that is referred to in it. Let the Holy Spirit convince you of these precious truths, Himself.

Walk with me into the corridors of the spirit ...the things I will share are not new, they have always existed in the Bible. It is the glory of God to conceal a matter, but the honor of kings to search out a thing! As you journey through this book, some things may seem a little unfamiliar. However, one thing is certain they will be scriptural.

CHAPTER 2
3 THINGS GOD IS

In the misty distance, the horizon seemed to clasp the icy waters in a tender embrace. Gleaming yellowish-brown light, the reflection of the rays of the rising sun, seemed to make a highway in the midst of the shimmering sea. Nature's fighter pilots – the sea gulls, were banking in tight curves, diving at impossible angles.... the sky, their ancient playground, these winged otters of the planet earth.

My eyes drank in this breath-taking scene, this orchestration of nature, such perfection, a flawless symphony, that only the master musician could have composed. There seemed no mistake, no error, only perfection. A perfect painting, by a perfect God, on the canvas of eternity.

God is perfect... excellent. And His excellence is reflected in His word.

At a point in my life, I caught the revelation of the excellency of wisdom. So great was the revelation, that an unusual hunger to walk in the fullness of wisdom engulfed my soul. The book of Proverbs became my dwelling place... what a hunger took me over! As I devoured the pages of the Bible, I discovered some things that sent my old theology out through the window.

First, I discovered that wisdom was much more than just a supernatural ability within a man. Actually, by definition, wisdom is God's ability within a man to rightly apply the knowledge that he has. Knowledge alone is of limited use. Yes, you know (knowledge), that Jesus heals, but it's possible you may still get sick and end up taking many drugs, and land in a hospital bed. The problem is not that you don't have knowledge; the problem is that you lack the ability to rightly apply the knowledge that you have. It is this ability to apply knowledge correctly that we call wisdom. It is the principal thing.

This truth is the same thing in finances,

relationships, spiritual growth, ministry etc. It is good to have knowledge in these areas, but better still, is the ability to *rightly apply the knowledge.*

GUESS WHAT?

However, I discovered that wisdom was more than the operation of a supernatural ability or a process. I discovered that wisdom is a person. I will not go into great depth concerning the revelation of wisdom, but there are some vital things that you must know:

GOD IS THREE THINGS:
(i) GOD IS LOVE
> *He that loveth not knoweth not God; for GOD IS LOVE.* **(1 John. 4 v 8)**

(ii) GOD IS LIFE
> *…. I am the way, the truth and the* **LIFE:** *no man cometh unto the father, but by me.* **(John. 14 v 6)**

(iii) GOD IS LIGHT
> *This then is the message which we have heard of him, and declare unto you,*

> that **GOD IS LIGHT**, *and in him is no*
> *darkness at all.* **(1 John. 1 v 5).**

LOVE, LIFE and LIGHT ...

Let's focus on the word "LIGHT".

This word **LIGHT** in **I John. 1 v 5** means **ILLUMINATION**. It goes beyond light produced from electricity, or the burning brightness of the sun.

This ILLUMINATION can be broken up into three:

(i) SIGHT

(ii) INSIGHT

(iii) FORESIGHT

SIGHT

This is the ability to SEE.

Do you remember Elisha's prayer for his servant, when they were surrounded by enemies?

> *And Elisha prayed, and said, LORD, I*
> *pray thee, OPEN his eyes, that he may*
> *SEE. And the LORD opened the eyes*

of the young man; AND HE SAW: **(2 kings. 6 v 17)**

There was "spiritual reality" present that Elisha was keenly aware of, that his servant knew nothing about. (read the entire story in **2 kings. 6 v 8 – 23**) God could have opened a door of opportunity for so many people, but there are those who will NOT SEE IT.

When Mary Magdalene saw the gardener on the resurrection morning, she did not **SEE** that it was the LORD, who she was searching for. Sometimes the blessing you have been crying for, could be dressed up like a poor wretched gardener!!

> *Jesus saith unto her, Woman, why weepiest thou? Whom seekest thou?* *She,* **SUPPOSING HIM TO BE THE GARDENER**, *saith unto him, Sir, if thou have borne him hence, tell me where thou hast laid him, and I will take him away.* **(John. 20 v 15).**

Can you believe that? The very person she was **WEEPING** for, was talking to her, and she **SUPPOSED HE WAS THE GARDENER.**

The ability to **SEE.**

When God brought Eve to Adam, he **recognized** her, though he had never **met** her before.

> *And Adam said, This is now bone of my*
> *bones, and flesh of my flesh: she shall be*
> *called Woman, because she was taken*
> *out of Man.* **(Genesis. 2 v 23).**

Can you imagine how many young men walked past the very woman that would have made a perfect wife, and **never knew it.** The ability to **SEE.** You have been praying for **open doors,** but when they come, will you SEE THEM? Child of God, why don't you bow your head right now and pray that God will open your eyes to *SEE all that you need to SEE, to be all that HE (GOD) wants you to be.*

Make this prayer a daily of yours, your life will never remain the same.

INSIGHT

This is the ability to see beyond the CONTAINER, into the CONTENT that it carries.

Never forget what I will write next... THE TRUE VALUE OF ANYTHING IS **INTERNAL** not **EXTERNAL.** When a person is walking in this ILLUMINATION of God, he will see a **smiling friendly face** and still be able to discern hatred and animosity hidden behind the smiling friendly **mask.** There is a difference between the **content** and the **container.** The **container** may look so sweet and beautiful. But hidden **INSIDE** this beautiful container could be the deadliest poison. A man of **INSIGHT** sees beyond the **container** into the **content.** That old saying is very true.... *It's not all that glitters that is gold.*

INSIGHT is deeper than SIGHT.

INSIGHT has to do with INTERPRETATION.

We have three things...

(i)   **Knowledge:**

This is the *acquiring* of facts.

(ii)   **Understanding:**

This is the *interpretation* of facts.

(iii)   **Wisdom:**

This is the *application* of facts.

A person of **INSIGHT** sees beyond the surface. Such a person will **discern motives** and **intents of the heart.**

A bottle of coca cola could look very attractive, with bright red and white markings. But at the end of the day, I am **not** going to drink the glass bottle which constitutes the "container", I am going to drink the liquid inside the container which constitutes the "content".

> *But the LORD said unto Samuel,* ***L O O K   N O T   O N   H I S   COUNTENANCE,*** *or on the* ***HEIGHT OF HIS STATURE;*** *because I have refused him: for the LORD seeth not as man seeth; for man looketh on the* ***OUTWARD APPEARANCE*** *but the LORD looketh on the* ***HEART.*** **(1 Samuel. 16 v 7).**

Samuel the tremendous Prophet, was looking at the **CONTAINER...** God had to caution him.

...Look not on his countenance.

3 Things God Is   19

While Samuel had his eyes on the **CONTAINER,** God had His eyes on the **CONTENT.**

...but the LORD LOOKETH ON THE HEART.

Even anointed prophetic ministries can be wrong! If Samuel's initial judgment had been followed, David would never have been anointed King.

FORESIGHT

This element will separate the **"MEN"** from the **"BOYS"**. **FORESIGHT** has to do with **"SEEING AHEAD"**. It is the ability to **PREDICT** situations, circumstances, future trends and events. A person of **FORESIGHT** will **not** be caught unawares. He or she will prepare adequately for an event before it occurs.

The person of foresight will **"meet"** a day, before it **"comes alive"**. By **FORESIGHT**, the signs of the coming times and the nudging's of the Spirit are analyzed and understood for fruitful action. People of **FORESIGHT** become **LEADERS.** They will be hurled head-first unto the pedestal of authority.

> *And of the children of Issachar, which were*
>
> *Men that had* **UNDERSTANDING OF THE TIMES,** *to know what Israel* **OUGHT TO DO...."**   **(1Chronicles.12v32A)**

The latter part of this verse says....

> *... and all their brethren were at their* **COMMANDMENT."**

THE CASE STATED

When a person has SIGHT, INSIGHT, and FORESIGHT, then that individual has **WISDOM.**

These three abilities: Sight, Insight and Foresight will fill a man with the **ability** to know **(1) What to do (2) How to do it (3) When to do it...** This is **WISDOM.**

Therefore, the LIGHT that is spoken about in **1 John 1 v 5** is **WISDOM. GOD IS LIGHT (WISDOM).**

CHAPTER 3

THE PERSON CALLED WISDOM

It's important that you realize that every member of the "GODHEAD" ... the Father, the Son and the Spirit... are ONE. There is no competition between them. The voice of any member of the Trinity, authoritatively represents the voice of the other two. They are in absolute agreement with each other.

The Holy Spirit will never say anything contrary to what Jesus or the Father is saying. They walk in an unbreakable unity. In the book of Revelations, we see an interesting truth revealed. In the portions of scripture that contain the letters to the seven churches in Asia Minor, you will discover a revelation of the unity displayed in the Trinity.

Let me show you the beginning and conclusion of just ONE of the Seven letters...

> *"And to the angel of the church in Philadelphia write; these things saith he that is holy, he that is true, he that hath the key of David, he that openeth, and no man shutteth; and shutteth, and no man openeth"* **(Revelations 3v7)**

The scripture above is the "beginning" of the letter to the church in Philadelphia. The letter starts off with JESUS speaking...

...these things saith he that is holy, he that is true...

However, the letter ends in a different way!

> *He that hath an ear, let him hear what the SPIRIT saith unto the churches.* **(Revelations 3v13)**

Did you see that?

Jesus starts the letter... but the letter ends with the Holy Spirit! Do you understand? They are one. They are in perfect unity and harmony. The voice of Jesus is the voice of the Holy Spirit. Whatever Jesus says, is what the Holy Spirit will say.

ONE, YET DIFFERENT

From the Bible we can see that even though the members of the Trinity are "ONE", each still differs from the other in the various ROLES that they each play.

One particular scripture that highlights their differences is found in Mathew chapter 3 v 16, 17:

> *And JESUS, when he was baptized, went up straightway out of the water: and, lo, the heavens were opened unto him, and he saw the SPIRIT OF GOD descending like a dove, and lighting upon him: And lo a VOICE from heaven, saying, This is my beloved Son, in whom I am well pleased.* **(Mathew 3v16,17)**

Here the scriptures reveal three distinct personalities, each performing different roles. One of them can be seen walking upon the earth and eventually comes to the Jordan and is baptized. Another is seen descending from heaven after the baptism and rests definitely upon the one that has been baptized. And yet another can be seen speaking from heaven about the one that was baptized.

This is supreme proof that three distinct personalities make up the Godhead. I did <u>not</u> say there are three Gods! There is ONE God, who is manifested in three distinct divine personalities: the Father, the Son and the Spirit.

OF DOVES AND LAMBS

Even though all the members of the Godhead were involved in the work of Redemption, each had a specific role to play. When John the Baptist saw Jesus, he made a unique pronouncement...

> *The next day John seeth JESUS coming unto him, and saith, Behold the LAMB OF GOD, which taketh away the sin of the world.* **(John. 1v 29)**

And again,

> *Neither is there SALVATION in any other: for there is none other NAME under heaven given among men, whereby we must be saved* **(Acts. 4v12)**

Now, even though we can "generally" say that "God" came down to earth and died for the sins of mankind, the truth is that it was "specifically" JESUS that came down to earth, represented the Trinity, and died for mankind. You see, each member of the Trinity has specific roles to play. You must understand the difference between a "general" reference and a "specific" assignment. The Holy Spirit was not the "lamb of God" that took away the sins of the world, it was Jesus.

WISDOM

In the same way, even though we can "generally" say that every member of the Godhead is WISDOM, there is however a particular individual among the Trinity who is known as the Spirit of WISDOM. When you encounter verses of the scripture like... Luke. 2 v 40 and Luke. 2v52... you will understand that JESUS Himself was under the intoxicating influence of this PERSON called WISDOM.

> *And the child grew, and waxed strong in spirit, FILLED WITH WISDOM: and the grace of God was upon him.*
> **(Luke 2v40)**

Then again,

> *And JESUS increased in WISDOM
> and stature, and in favor with God and
> man.* **(Luke 2v52)**

LETS GO DEEPER

Isaiah declares in the 11th chapter, the 1st and 2nd verses:

> *And there shall come forth a rod out of
> the stem of Jesse, and a Branch shall
> grow out of his roots:*
>
> *And the spirit of the LORD shall rest
> upon him, the spirit of WISDOM and
> understanding, the spirit of counsel
> and might, the spirit of knowledge and
> of the fear of the LORD;* **(Isaiah.
> 11v1,2)**

The scriptures above are a prophecy concerning the Lord Jesus. The second verse of Isaiah eleven reveals various attributes of the Holy Spirit that was to REST UPON JESUS. One of those attributes was: THE SPIRIT OF WISDOM. The Holy Spirit is the "SPIRIT OF WISDOM" In Deuteronomy 34v49 we encounter the "Spirit of wisdom" again:

And Joshua the son of Nun was full of the SPIRIT OF WISDOM; for Moses had laid his hands upon him: and the children of Israel hearkened unto him and did as the LORD commanded Moses. **(Deuteronomy 34v9)**

Moses could only impart what he himself possessed. Through the vehicle of the laying on of hands, the spirit and anointing upon Moses was transferred into the life of Joshua. Some people may argue and say… "the Spirit of wisdom spoken about here is not referring to the Holy Spirit but to the divine faculty of "WISDOM" … My answer to this statement is…. "That functional ability in a man's life called WISDOM can only be present because of the presence of the Holy Spirit. It is the presence of the Spirit that brings the wisdom of God into a man. The person called WISDOM releases a supernatural ability called "wisdom".

HANG ON!

But the book of Proverbs went a step further…WISDOM is a PERSON… YES, BUT NOT JUST A PERSON! The book of Proverbs calls WISDOM A WOMAN!

CHAPTER 4

WHEN WISDOM IS
A WOMAN

Wisdom crieth without; **SHE** *uttered* **HER** *voice in the streets:* **SHE** *crieth in the chief place of concourse, in the openings of the gates; in the city* **SHE** *uttereth* **HER** *words, saying...*
(Proverbs 1v20,21)

In this chapter we are going to come face to face with a scriptural reality that is amazing. The book of **Proverbs** throws light on this PERSON that is called WISDOM. Here in **Proverbs** the veil is removed from WISDOM'S face and we have a clearer view. The book of **Proverbs** refers to WISDOM as a **WOMAN**

DID YOU REALISE?

It was no mistake by the translators of the Bible... God by **"divine design"**, allowed WISDOM to be referred to as a **WOMAN**.

Say unto Wisdom, thou art my **SISTER:** *and call understanding thy* **KINSWOMAN.** **(Proverbs 7v4)**

And again,

WISDOM hath builded **HER** house, **SHE** hath hewn out **HER** seven pillars **SHE** hath killed **HER** beasts; **SHE** hath mingled **HER** wine; **SHE** hath also furnished **HER** table. **(Proverbs 9v1,2)**

Even in the Gospels... the very last part of verse **nineteen** of **Mathew chapter eleven:**

...But **WISDOM** *is justified of* **HER** *children.* **(Mathew 11v19b)**

Dear reader, my prayer for you at this point is that you will be able to catch deep in your heart the amazing revelation of an aspect of the Holy Spirit's personality that has the explosive potential of revolutionizing your entire life.

THE HOLY SPIRIT IS WISDOM PERSONIFIED, AND THIS PERSON CALLED WISDOM IS REFERRED TO AS A **WOMAN.**

SCRIPTURAL PROOF

From studying the Bible about man's creation, it is clear that Adam got his masculine characteristics from God. Now, where do you think Eve got her feminine characteristics from? Well, Eve got her feminine characteristics from God as well. God has both **masculine** and **feminine** characteristics.

Eve **did not** get her feminine characteristics from the devil... NO...She got them from God.

ELOHIM

In the Book of **Genesis,** in the **first chapter,** we catch a glimpse of the summary of the creation of the planet earth and the genesis of mankind...

In the **26th verse** the scripture declares...

> And **GOD** said, Let **US** make man in our image, after our likeness: and let them have dominion over the fish of the sea, and over the fowl of the air, and over the cattle, and over all the earth,

and over every creeping thing that creepeth upon the earth. **(Genesis 1v26)**

The Hebrew word that is translated **GOD** in **Genesis 1v26,** is the word **ELOHIM.** It is the same Hebrew word that is translated "**GOD**" in **Genesis. 1v1.** It can also be spelt **ELOHIM.** There are two important characteristics attached to the name **ELOHIM.**

The first is that ELOHIM is **PLURAL.**

And God (ELOHIM) said, Let **US** *make man in* **OUR** *image...*

The **Dake's annotated Reference Bible** gives the following information:

Two names of God prove Plurality of persons.The Heb. ELOHIM is the word for God in Genesis 1v1, and in over 2,700 other places in the Old Testament. It is a uniplural noun meaning Gods and is so translated 239 time[1].

ELOHIM is a name that indicates God's power and preeminence.

The Hebrew and Chaldee dictionary of **the Strong's Exhaustive Concordance,** gives the information that the word **ELOHIM,** is the **PLURAL** form of the word **ELOAH²**. It can also be spelt **ELOAHH**. So, the word ELOAH is the singular form of the word ELOHIM.

> *"And GOD (ELOHIM) said, Let US make man..."*

The word **ELOHIM,** which is translated **GOD** in <u>Genesis 1v1</u> and <u>Genesis.1v26</u> is referring to **three** divine personalities; The **Father,** the **Son,** and the **Holy Spirit.** Actually, each member of the "GODHEAD", Contributed to the creation of the "person" they were creating.

The **Second** characteristic about ELOHIM that we will deal with in this book, is the fact that ELOHIM is both **masculine and feminine.**

So, God (ELOHIM) created man in his own image, in the image of God created he him; **MALE** and **FEMALE** created he them. (Genesis 1v27)

Once again, as in **Genesis 1v1 and 26,** the Hebrew word for God in **Genesis 1v27** is the word **ELOHIM.**

CHAPTER 5
THE SYMBOL OF MOTHERHOOD

A careful study of spiritual and physical laws, events and creations, will force one to admit that the physical world in which we live with its laws, events and creations was definitely *patterned* after the realm of the spirit.

PHYSICAL THINGS are a copy of **SPIRITUAL ORIGINALS**. **Fatherhood, Motherhood** and **Family life** is a copy of a **SPIRITUAL ORIGINAL**.

Family life exists in the realm of the spirit.

Of whom the whole FAMILY in HEAVEN and earth is named, **(Ephesians 3v15)**

The Scripture above shows us that there is a

heavenly family (a spiritual family). **"Fatherhood"** and **"Motherhood"** exist in the realm of the Spirit as well. Just as there are physical "Fathers" on earth... God the Father, is the **spiritual** symbol of **fatherhood.** Jesus, among other things, stands as a **spiritual symbol** of an **offspring.**

Have you ever asked yourself WHO THE SYMBOL OF **MOTHERHOOD** IN THE TRINITY IS? I have shown you the **symbol** of FATHERHOOD in the Trinity... He is GOD the FATHER. I have shown you the **symbol** of an OFFSPRING in the Trinity... He is GOD the SON.

And now from clear scriptural proof, you will see that the Holy Spirit is the **symbol** of **MOTHERHOOD** in the Trinity.

IN THE MOUTH OF TWO OR THREE

In Genesis chapter 1v2 we see something exciting:

> *And the earth was without form and void; and darkness was upon the face of the deep. And the **Spirit** of God MOVED upon the face of the waters.*

The word, "**MOVED**", here in this scripture, is used to describe the action of the Holy Spirit upon the waters. The word, "**MOVED**", is translated from the Hebrew word **RACHAPH.** The Hebrew word **RACHAPH** means to "**BROOD**" or to "**INCUBATE**". It refers to the action a "MOTHER HEN" or "CHICKEN" performs on her eggs, to get them to hatch.

The Holy Spirit is the symbol of MOTHERHOOD... it is his job to "BROOD" or "INCUBATE" the "**eggs**" or "**seed**" of the spirit realm, just like a "Mother hen", so that they will hatch.

...look at a mystery...

> *And in the sixth month the angel Gabriel was sent from God unto a city of Galilee, named Nazareth.* (**Luke 1v26**)

> *To a virgin espoused to a man whose name was Joseph, of the house of David; and the Virgin's name was Mary.* (**Luke 1v27**)

> *And the angel said unto her, Fear not,*

*Mary: for thou hast found favor with
God.* **(Luke. 1v30)**

*And, behold, thou shall conceive in
thy womb, and bring forth a son, and
shalt call his name JESUS* **(Luke
1v30,31)**

When the angel Gabriel appeared to Mary
and gave her this message from God, she was
troubled. She instantly began to reason along
physical lines and saw the physical limitations
to this incredible promise.

*Then said Mary unto the angel, **How
shall this be,** seeing I know not a
man?* **(Luke 1v34)**

Mary rightly realized that from the
physical standpoint this promise was
impossible. Biologically speaking, she had to
have sexual intercourse with a man for her to
become pregnant. But God had His plan:

*And the angel answered and said unto
her, The **HOLY GHOST** shall **COME
UPON THEE,** and the power of the
Highest shall overshadow thee:*

therefore also that holy thing which shall be born of thee shall be called the Son of God. **(Luke 1v35)**

God the "FATHER" had a plan to plant the **incorruptible seed (THE WORD)** into Mary's womb...

Being born again, not of ***CORRUPTIBLE SEED,*** *but of* ***INCORRUPTIBLE,*** *by the* ***WORD OF GOD,*** *which liveth and abideth for ever.* **(1 Peter 1v23)**

THE WORD IS THE SEED.

God planned that this SEED or WORD in the womb of Mary would grow and develop and...

... the WORD was made flesh, and dwelt among us, (and we beheld his glory, the glory as of the ***ONLY BEGOTTEN*** *of the* ***FATHER,)*** *full of grace and truth.* **(John 1v14)**

Halleluyah!

God knew that Mary physically did not have the equipment to conceive and nurture this spiritual entity in her womb, so he told her...*Please allow me to paraphrase what the angel told Mary in Luke. 1v35, in my own words:*

> ... *"the angel answered and said to her (Mary), I know by your human power or ability you cannot conceive or nurture this spiritual entity that is to be born into the world through you...But don't worry, the Holy Spirit... the* **SYMBOL OF MOTHERHOOD** *shall* **COME UPON YOU,** *His power will overshadow you. It will not be you (Mary) doing the nurturing in the womb-this is a* **spiritual operation** *– it will be the Holy Spirit doing it-all you have to be is a channel. He is the one who will do the job of* **INCUBATING,** *for the "WORD", or the SEED of Hatch".*

Just as He (the Holy Spirit) **brooded** or **incubated** over the waters in **Genesis chapter 1,** He also came to incubate over Mary and the SEED planted in her womb.

HE IS THE SYMBOL OF MOTHERHOOD!

THE PARAKLETOS

And I will pray the Father, and he shall give you another **COMFORTER,** *that he may abide with you forever;* **(John. 14 v 16)**

The Comforter being spoken about in this scripture, is the Holy Spirit. The Greek word that is translated COMFORTER in **John. 14 v 16,** is the word **PARAKLETOS...** it means, **"one called to one's side to give aid".** The word PARAKLETOS is very rich with a variety of meanings. However, one word that sums up the meaning of the word very well, is the English word "COMFORTER". The word PARAKLETOS can also be translated Counselor, Helper, Advocate, Strengthener, Intercessor, and Standby.

Take a look at this scripture that further confirms the fact that the Holy Spirit is the symbol of Motherhood.

And Isaac brought her into his mother Sarah's tent, and took Rebecca, and **SHE** *became his* **WIFE;** *and he loved* *her: and   Isaac was* **COMFORTED** *after his mother's Death.* **(Genesis. 24 v 67).**

WOW! did you see that?

When Rebecca became Isaac's wife something unique happened... He (Isaac) was **COMFORTED** Isaac was **COMFORTED** ONLY **AFTER** Rebecca (woman) came into his life and became is wife. A woman has the God-given ministry of the comforter. This is the ministry of the Holy Spirit...the ministry of the **comforter.**

CHAPTER 6

SIX DOORS

And I will pray the Father, and he shall give you another COMFORTER, that he may abide with you forever; **(John. 14 v 16)**

The young man walked down the narrow hallway with measured steps, the thick plush carpet, muting the sound of his immaculate shoes. He was impeccably dressed in a grey three-piece suit. His crisp white shirt made a handsome background for his blue hand-woven tie. He cut a picture of wealth, confidence and success.

He gazed at the large, framed photographs that lined each wall of the narrow hallway. As his eyes roved over each picture, his heart swelled with pride, his eyes brimming with tears. These were his ancestors. These were the men and women whose blood flowed in his veins. People that sowed their sweat, tears, blood and lives to create this legendary financial empire that he had been born into.

Ten years ago, his father had walked down this hallway holding his hand. He had paused at each picture and told his son... his heir, the "tales of old". For three hours, he listened to the dreams, the ambitions, the struggles, the achievements, the betrayals and the mistakes of his ancestors. When his father was through, he felt strangely different... awed. The men he once scorned, he now revered. And now, ten years later, on a cold December night, he once again walked starry eyed, through the "hall of fame", pausing every little while to relive the melodies of the ancient past. Time could not erase his fathers last statement that night ten years ago... he said...

> *"Son, this is the legacy our ancestors left us, never lower this noble standard, never corrupt these lofty ideals. It's your turn now son,*

remember the family tradition, don't bring shame into your inheritance" ...

In another place, at another time, twelve men sat huddled together in the biting cold. They trembled, not because of the cold, but because of fear. Their world seemed to be crumbling around them. Dark clouds of uncertainty seemed to gather. There was a cold stick feeling in the pit of their stomachs. The one who calmed the raging sea was leaving. The one who fed multitudes with one little boy's lunch was saying goodbye. In a flash, they remembered the way the demons had screamed out of the madman of the Gadarenes, with one command from the master. They remembered the healing stream of virtue that flowed from Emmanuel's hands.... Healing the sick, raising the dead, cleansing the lepers... they remembered...

In a moment, tears began to trickle gently, reluctantly down their faces. These rugged fisherman, hardened tax collectors, one-time skeptics. The reality that Jesus was really going away had finally dawned on them. They sat down in a semi circle, their strong rugged arms clasped around their knees, their eyes filled with their pain, staring ahead into nothingness. And then in that moment, with their hearts overwhelmed with grief, the most compassionate man history ever knew, stretched forth his healing hands, and with a voice laced with emotion, we hear him say...

... And I will pray the Father and He will give you another Comforter...

He was placing into their hands a timeless legacy. A legacy that would outlive them and span the ages to come. He had passed on to them and indeed to all that would come to the saving knowledge of Christ, the legacy of the eternal Spirit.

In the last chapter we dealt with the Greek word **PARAKLETOS** which is translated **COMFORTER** in **John 14 v 16.** We also saw six other words that could equally be translated Parakletos: **Counselor, Helper, Advocate, Strengthener, Intercessor** and **Standby.** A careful study of these six words reveals a **similarity** between the role of the Holy Spirit in the life of a person, and the role of a woman.

Let's take a journey together, let's knock upon **six doors**...

.... HELPER...

God declared in Genesis chapter 2v18

> *And the Lord God said, it is not good that the man should be alone; I will make him a **HELP MEET** for him.*

God created the woman to be a helper for the man. This is the ministry of the Holy Spirit... "THE HELPER".

...STANDBY...

A perfect day, the sun is shining outside, the birds are singing, the pipe organ is booming in the little Methodist Church... a gentle voice is heard echoing the words of the officiating minister...

..."*to love and to cherish, till death do us part, according to God's Holy law*"

The tail end of the typical marriage vow. A woman is supposed to STANDBY her husband forever, till death or rapture parts them. She must stand with him in wind and storm, when he's right and when he's wrong... if she leaves, who then does he have to lean on? This is the ministry of the Spirit... "THE STANDBY", a present help in the time of trouble.

...STRENGTHENER...

I left her presence "ten feet taller", it seemed as if the sun itself was shining at full strength inside me... my once hunched shoulders now straight and square. I felt like a man. I felt like a winner... the head that once sagged in defeat and disgrace now lifted with pride, with strength, with courage.

Overnight, I became like an emperor, like a swooping eagle. My close friends were shocked at the change in me! I had just had a divine encounter with the ministry of the **strengthener** in the life of a woman. She wasn't a preacher, just a simple saint... it wasn't so much the words she said, but the atmosphere she brought. She didn't preach any sermon, but as we shared about our favorite Bible passages, our mistakes, our victories, the hunger of our hearts... God's throne seemed to descend. Every word she said seemed to echo... "I have faith in you", "You can make it", "I'm proud of you".

WOMAN, you can set "his" soul on fire with a courage and determination the world has rarely seen... or you can break his spirit, leaving him wounded and limping!

Remember the story of Samson and Delilah? When the Philistine Lords discovered a smoldering love affair between Samson and Delilah, they approached her and bargained with her to be a doorway for his destruction **(Judges. 16v4-5)** ... Daily, she asked him for the secret of his great strength, that he might be destroyed.

> *...And it came to pass, when she pressed him daily with her* **WORDS,** *and* **URGED** *him, so that his* **SOUL WAS VEXED UNTO DEATH** *...* **(Judges. 16v16)**

In the spirit things work in one of two directions. Things will either work positively or negatively. The one who has the role of the "strengthener" can yield to the devil and be used as the "weakener".

WOMAN... maybe you didn't know it, but your continual nagging has "vexed his soul unto death" ... instead of infusing him with divine ability, you have drained him of even his last reserves!

You have in your tongue the ability to lift his sagging frame with life and energy, courage and faith in himself... to fire his spirit with such dauntless ambition that he screams before every circumstance and situation... "I am an overcomer"!

Again, this is the ministry of the Spirit... "THE STRENGTHENER".

...ADVOCATE...

An advocate is someone like a lawyer... one who will stand between you and another person or a multitude and **speak in your favor, plead your case** before the judge, who has the power to pass the death sentence. An Advocate will defend you and struggle to cause all danger, harm, disadvantage and inconvenience to be diverted away from you. Many a time a man was destined for the gallows, the noose of the hangman, but the brilliance of his lawyer's defense kept him alive. A classic case of a woman standing as an **advocate** is demonstrated in the actions of **Abigail** the wife of Nabal in **1 Samuel 25v1-35.**

At a point in time, during the forced exile of David, when he fled from King Saul, he dwelt for a period in the wilderness of Paran with his band of valiant warriors **(1 Samuel. 25v1).** During his exile he encountered the flocks and herds of a very great man called Nabal (Abigail's Husband). David, instead of stealing out of these great flocks or even destroying them, guarded them and protected them from dangers (both natural and man-made) **- 1 Samuel. 25v15,16.**

David could have taken any amount of sheep and goat from Nabal by force and fed his men, but he decided to ask Nabal's permission....

I give, I pray thee, whatsoever cometh to thine hand unto thy servants, and to thy son David. **(I Samuel. 25v8b)**

Nabal, a devil of a man, sent a nasty refusal back to David, an insult thrown into the monarch's face. David became angry and passed the death sentence on Nabal.

When Abigail heard of her husband's vile conduct and David's death sentence, she moved to intercept David, in a desperate bid to avert the imminent bloodshed.

> *And David said to Abigail, Blessed be the LORD God of Israel, which sent thee this day to meet me:*
>
> *And blessed be **THY ADVICE**. and blessed be thou, which hast kept me this day from coming to shed blood, and from avenging myself with my own hand.*
>
> *For in very deed, as the Lord God of Israel liveth, which hath kept me back from hurting thee, **EXCEPT THOU HADST HASTED AND COME TO MEET ME,** surely there had not been left unto Nabal by the morning light any that pisseth against the wall* **(1 Samuel. 25v32)**

This noble action of hers, forever puts Abigail in the hall of fame of historic events.

Massive destruction was averted, because Abigail took on the ministry of the **advocate,** and **pleaded the case** of Nabal. This also is the ministry of the Holy Spirit... "THE ADVOCATE".

...INTERCESSOR...

If anything characterizes the life of a wife and mother in the Body of Christ, it is **intercession...** she watches over her husband and children in intercession.

Intercession can be broken up into two categories... (i) Intercessory prayer and (ii) intercessory action. We must learn to talk to God about people, before we talk to people about God. The intercessor goes to God on behalf of a person, a people or a situation... intercession is not done for oneself, but it is done on behalf of another.

WOMAN, you play a crucial role, a vital part in the life of your husband, children and the body of Christ. Your children will begin to see your husband through your eyes... they will see people, actions and events through your eyes...

So, cleanse your eyes, let them not be eyes of contempt, of scorn, of evil…

> …*Behold, everyone that useth proverbs shall use this proverb against thee, saying,* **As is the mother, so is her daughter.** **(Ezekiel. 16v44)**

You have the power to influence your children towards God or away from God:

> …*When I call to remembrance the unfeigned faith that is in thee, which* ***DWELT FIRST IN THY GRANDMOTHER LOIS,*** *and thy* ***MOTHER EUNICE;*** *and I am persuaded that in thee* ***ALSO.*** **(II Timothy 1v5)**

As physical traits, like height, complexion and voice similarities are passed on to children from their parents, through genes and association, also, spiritual traits and qualities can be passed on to children by parents. This was the case with Timothy. With the wisdom of God flowing through a WOMAN, she can build such a "Spirit" into a child that the earth will marvel at such a marvelous manifestation of the "divine idea". Have you ever stopped to wonder what kind of a woman Adolf Hitler's mother was? A woman that produced a man, that is remembered for the evil he did!

Dear woman, as your rock that cradle, as you nurse that child, you have an opportunity to give mankind another Apostle Paul, another Joseph Ayo Babalola another John Wesley, another Maria Woodworth Etter. Once again, this is also the ministry of the Spirit of God... "THE INTERCESSOR". Let's knock on the last door...

...COUNSELOR...

One of the main problem areas in any marriage and relationship is **communication.**   Other problem areas revolve around **sex** and **money.** The problems found in any relationship will most likely be from one of these areas.

WOMAN... you are more than a baby factory... you should be your husband's best friend, the first person he speaks to, about pressing issues on his mind... his confidant. A woman has an unusual ability to affect the life of a man! She can **make** or **mar** him.

Lack of **communication** has been the death of many marriages. The counselor is one who communicates advice on the course of action to take, or the direction in which to move. The Counselor tries to put the **distorted picture** into the right perspective, for positive fruitful action.

Let's see the incredible results of the counsel of a woman from the pages of the Bible. In the book of Genesis, we come in contact with a unique story that is a brilliant example of the positive power of a woman's **counsel.** The story of **Rebecca** and her timely counsel to her son Jacob has been highlighted from various pulpits in a **negative** way. It has been seen as the action and counsel of a woman under a generational curse of "deception", which was apparent in Laban her brother, and her favorite son Jacob. However, as I studied the Bible, I began to see the **positive** sides of Rebecca's COUNSEL to Jacob in **Genesis 27v5-13.** When you go back to the manner in which Rebecca was selected to be Isaac's wife, you will realize she was divinely chosen for Isaac by God. Read the entire story of her selection in **Genesis 24v1-67.**

If Isaac had been allowed to release the

blessing of God into Esau his favorite son's life, it would have been a **great mistake,** because even before the two boys were born, it had been decided who would be the leader.

> *And the LORD said unto her, Two nations are in thy womb, and two manner of people shall be separated from thy bowels; and the one people shall be stronger than the other people;* **and THE ELDER SHALL SERVE THE YOUNGER (Genesis. 25:23)**

Years ago, I came across a scripture that I battled with. It seemed to contradict the nature of God I had known. This scripture seemed to contradict scriptures like...

> *Thou lovest righteousness, and hatest wickedness: therefore God, thy God, hath anointed thee with the oil of gladness above thy fellows.* **(Psalm 45v7)**

The scripture above from **Psalm 45v7** proves that there is a **reason** for every **blessing.** I came to learn that there is a difference between the **"LOVE"** of God, and the **"BLESSING"** of God. We can do **nothing** to earn God's **LOVE** us no matter what we **have done or will ever do.** The Bible declares...

> *But God commendeth his **LOVE** toward us, in that, while we were **YET SINNERS,** Christ died for us.* **(Romans 5v8).**

However, the BLESSING of God is different. God's BLESSING does NOT come simply because He LOVES you, God's BLESSING comes into a person's life because of OBEDIENCE.

> *And all these **BLESSING** shall **COME** on thee, and OVERTAKE thee, if thou shall **HEARKEN UNTO THE VOICE OF THE LORD THY GOD.*** **(Deuteronomy 28v2)**

Now as I wrote earlier, I came across a scripture that I struggled with. This is the scripture...

*As it is written, Jacob have **I LOVED,** but Esau have I **HATED** (Roman 9v13)*

When I read this scripture, somehow, I just could not accept that a **JUST, UPRIGHT** AND **PERFECT** God, could look at two UNBORN children and decide to show FAVOUR to one and HATRED to the other **for no reason.**

At times the **SINS** of a parent or an ancestor could launch a child into a lifetime of sorrow, as he or she battles with the fruit of an **inherited curse...** paying for a sin they did not commit.

For example, in **2 Kings 5,** we come in contact with the story of Gehazi the servant of Elisha the Prophet, who came under a **CURSE** from God because of his covetous lifestyle and hypocrisy. But the unfortunate thing was that he plunged his **family, for generations to come,** into the same CURSE he received.

*The leprosy therefore of Naaman shall cleave unto thee, **AND UNTO THY SEED FOR EVER.** And he went out from his presence a leper as white as snow.* **(2 Kings 5v27)**

Do you realize that except God removed the curse at some point in time, there is still someone on the earth **TODAY** that is a leper because of Gehazi? The curse was to affect **UNBORN GENERATIONS... FOREVER!**

So, when God said in **Romans. 9v13...**

> *...Jacob have I loved, but Esau have I hated.*

He had a **reason** why He made this statement. Doesn't it make you feel **insecure** if you served a God that could decide to **HATE** and **AFFLICT** you tomorrow WITHOUT ANY **JUST CAUSE!** And when you ask Him why He is punishing you, He answers and says... **"I JUST FEEL LIKE DEALING WITH YOU THAT WAY TODAY"!**

God is **NOT** unpredictable... He will do what His WORD says He will do. This understanding is essential for spiritual progress.

TYPES AND SHADOWS

For if he were on earth, he should not be a priest, seeing that there are priests that offer gifts according to the law: Who serve unto the **EXAMPLE** AND **SHADOW** of heavenly things, as Moses was admonished of God when he was about to make the tabernacle: for, See, saith he, that thou make all things according to the pattern shewed to thee in the mount. (Hebrews 8v4,5)

The Old Testament is full of **types, shadows, examples, lessons** and **divine patterns,** that the Lord would want us to understand, decode, learn from and apply in our lives. I tell people over and over that Christianity is not a religion. Instead, Christianity is God's **idea** or **concept** of how man should **live** and **operate.** Christianity is more than a two- or three-hour service in a building that we call a church. It is the daily expression of the life indwelt by God in any place and at every time… this is Christianity.

God is full of concepts on how we should live and move and have our being. These divine concepts on the ideal lifestyle and the plans, purpose and agenda of God is packaged in a written from called the Bible.

TWO NATURES

The scriptures teach about the multisided, many faceted wisdom of God.

> *To the intent that now unto the principalities and powers in heavenly places might be known by the church the MANIFOLD wisdom of God* **(Ephesians 3v10)**

Just as God's wisdom has many sides, different characters and stories in the Bible teach many lessons for various situations. For instance, just one "parable" could be applied to different situations and seen from various "angles".

Apart from being two humans born into the earth at a point in time, ESAU and JACOB are definitely **symbolic** of certain things. When Rebecca the mother of the two boys, went to the Lord to enquire about the reason for her unusual pregnancy, she got a startling answer.

> *And the children struggled together within her; and she said, If it be so, why am I thus? And she went to enquire of the LORD* **(Genesis 25v22)**

Now her enquiry brought an unusual answer.

> *And the LORD said unto her, Two nations are in thy womb, and **TWO MANNER** of people shall be separated from thy bowels; and the one people shall be stronger than the other people; and **THE ELDER SHALL SERVE THE YOUNGER*** (Genesis 25v23)

ESUA and JACOB are **symbolic** of two natures in the life of the **believer:**

1. THE FLESH
2. THE SPIRIT

The struggle that went on in Rebecca's womb is **symbolic** of a struggle that occurs at various points in the life of the believer.

> *For the **FLESH** lusted against the **SPIRIT**, and the **SPIRIT** against the **FLESH**: and these are contrary the one to the other: so that ye cannot do the things that ye would.* **(Galatians 5v17)**

Another translation reads,

> *For the **FLESH** sets its desire AGAINST the **SPIRIT**, and the **SPIRIT** against the **FLESH** for these are in OPPOSITION to one another, so that you may not do the things that you please.* **(Galatians 5v17, NAS).**

The term "FLESH" is the collective term for the **"FIVE SENSES"**. The **Five senses** are: 1. The sense of SIGHT   2. The sense of SMELL 3. The sense of HEARING   4. The sense of TASTE   5. The sense of TOUCH.

As you study the scriptures, you will realize that ESAU the FIRSTBORN of a set of twins, was a man of the FLESH, a man of the **senses.** He is symbolic of the FLESH. On the other hand, his younger brother JACOB, though not a perfect role model of society, is symbolic of the SPIRIT – **not** the "Holy Spirit", but the **"Human Spirit,"** that still needs to grow, develop and mature.

> *As **NEWBORN BABES** desire the sincere milk of the word, that ye may GROW thereby:* **(1 Peter. 2v2)**

ESAU and JACOB

And the boys grew: and Esau was a **CUNNING HUNTER,** *a man of the field; and Jacob was a* **PLAIN** *man, dwelling in tents.* **(Genesis 25v27).**

From the scriptures we can see that Esau was a rough, tough, uncultured man. He was a hunter, used to the Jungles and dense thickets. He was a man who was ready to **break away** from family values. This is demonstrated in the fact that when his grandfather, father and brother were men who tended **sheep** and reared **livestock,** he **broke away** and became a **hunter.**

His brother on the other hand was a sharp contrast to him. The scriptures tell us that Jacob was a **"PLAIN"** man. The word PLAIN is the Hebrew word **"TAM". TAM** means **"complete", "perfect", "undefiled", "upright".** These various translations of the word **TAM** remind one of the **fruit of the spirit.**

WHO CARES!

And Esau said, Behold, I am at the point to die: and **WHAT PROFIT SHALL THIS BIRTHRIGHT DO TO ME?** **(Genesis 25v32).**

Esau placed no value on his incredible, divine **birthright.** It was useless to him. He valued a "morsel of meat" more than the "blessing of God". This is the FLESH. The FLESH will long for satisfaction, even if the result is the damnation of your soul. The FLESH lives for the **moment** with no thought of the **future.**

If Esau could have sold his **birthright** to his brother in a desperate fit of hunger, then he could have sold it to any other person who was wise enough to have discerned it's value. The **works** of the FLESH don't bring peace of mind, rather they bring sorrow, heartache and regret. Esau's marriage to two particular women exemplifies the result of the works of the FLESH.

> *And Esau was forty years old when he took to wife Judith the daughter of Beeri the Hittite, and Bashemath the daughter of Elon the Hittite: Which were a **GRIEF OF MIND UNTO** Isaac and to Rebecca* **(Genesis 26v34,35)**

When the FLESH has its way, the result is GRIEF. I am of the opinion that Rebecca did humanity a **favor** by directing the blessing of God to the **right person.**

When a man is born again, he has a recreated spirit that never existed before. Now, the nature of the FLESH in this individual is, technically speaking, **older** than the newly recreated SPIRIT the man received when he got born again. This is the case in every person who gets born again! Your old FLESH nature is, technically speaking, older than the newly recreated SPIRIT you received at your new birth. So, when God said the ELDER will serve the YOUNGER, the statement was **symbolic** of how God has ordained that your **SPIRIT MAN** should RULE, CONTROL and DOMINATE YOUR **FLESH.**

The scripture in **Galatians. 6v8** was wonderfully fulfilled in positive dimensions, as the unique, strategic blessing was placed upon the shoulders of the rightful God ordained heir.

*For he that soweth to his **FLESH** shall*
*of the **FLESH** reap corruption; but he*
*that soweth to the **SPIRIT** shall of the*

SPIRIT reap life everlasting.
(Galatians 6v8)

Isaac almost SOWED the blessing to the FLESH. It was the **intervention** of Rebecca that saved the day. Today You and I who are believers and children of the kingdom, have reaped **life everlasting** through the blessing that Isaac finally SOWED to the RIGHT PERSON. Jesus came through the line of **Jacob** not **Esau.**

This is also the ministry of the Holy Spirit… "THE COUNSELLOR".

CHAPTER 7
HE OR SHE?

Writhing across the skies, like a snake in its death throes…like a heavenly stream running its phantom course, the lightning struck. Its downward plunge, like a plummeting eagle, bearing down relentlessly upon its prey. The skies lit up in a brief burst of silver pleasure. Here one moment, gone the next.

The lightning… so real and vibrant one moment, and then suddenly there's no trace it ever blazed a silver trail across the lonely sky. Don't let this book be one you will read once and forget about. Read it over and over. Let its message plunge into the depths of your heart. Don't let the revelation of this book blaze in your life with the briefness of flashing lightning… let it be an eternal fire raging in your soul.

Howbeit when **HE,** *the spirit of truth, is come,* **HE** *will guide you into all truth, for* **HE** *shall not speak of* **HIMSELF;** *but whatsoever* **HE** *shall hear, that shall* **HE** *speak: and* **HE** *will shew you things to come.* **(John. 16 v 13)**

As you read through this book, your mind has perhaps been assailed by a particular thought:

"If the Holy Spirit is indeed the symbol of **MOTHERHOOD** in the Trinity, why doesn't the Bible say **...Howbeit when "SHE"** the Spirit of truth is come"?

In the scripture written above, **John. 16 v 13,** the pronoun **"HE",** which in the Greek language is the word **EKEINOS,** is used over and over.

However, **W.E. Vines** brings out some important facts under his treatise of the word **"SPIRIT"** in his acclaimed book... **Vine's Expository Dictionary of old and New Testament Words:**

"The Personality of the Spirit is emphasized at the expense of strict grammatical procedure in

John. 14v26; 15:26; 16:8, 13, 14, `where the emphatic pronoun *ekeinos*, "**He**", is used of Him in the masculine, whereas the noun *pneuma* is neuter in Greek, while the corresponding word in Aramaic, the language in which our Lord probably spoke, is feminine (*rucha, cf. Heb. ruach*)"[3]

Let's focus on certain words W.E. VINE uses in the passage above that was extracted from his book.

(1) The word **PNEUMA**

(2) The word **RUACH**

The word **PNEUMA,** is the Greek equivalent to the English word **SPIRIT**. It is this word PNEUMA that is used in **John. 14v26; 15v26; 16v8, 13, 14.**

The word PNEUMA (SPIRIT) is **NEUTER,** in the Greek language. The term **NEUTER** means a class of words (especially nouns, pronouns, adjectives) not connected to **male** or **female** qualities. In other words, in the Greek language, the word PNEUMA does **not** have **male** or **female** qualities or suggestions... it is without **gender.**

However, what is perhaps most revealing is the fact that the corresponding **word** for SPIRIT in **ARAMAIC, is a FEMININE** word!

The New Revised Edition of the **CHAMBER'S ENCYCLOPEDIA** gives the following information:

Aramaic, originally the language of the Aramaeans, to whom reference is often made in the Assyrian records from the 12th century B.C. onwards, was probably the first language ever to become an important international tongue...

It displaced Hebrew among the Jews, probably from the 5th century B.C. onwards and was one of the two languages spoken by them (The other being Greek) in Palestine in New Testament times [4]

Now **W.E. VINE,** is careful to **suggest** in his treatise that it is a **possibility** that Jesus our Lord, spoke ARAMAIC!

However, **THE AMERICAN PEOPLES ENCYCLOPEDIA** is more certain:

Aramaic, an important branch of the Semitic languages in which are included Syria, Palestinian and biblical Aramaic, and Samaritan.

Jesus spoke Aramaic. *The writing on the wall seen by Belshazzar was in Aramaic. Aramaic is still* *spoken by Christians living on the border of Iraq and Iran and in some villages close to Damascus, in Syria.*[5]

Well dear reader, we can perhaps only make an educated guess... an assumption, about the language Jesus spoke. But whatever the case may be, the **fact** is that the corresponding word for Spirit in ARAMAIC is *feminine.*

And again...

The third edition of **The Cambridge Paper back Encyclopedia**, which was published in 1999, has this to say about ARAMAIC...

*...A Semitic language still spoken by small communities in the Middle East. **A dialect of Aramaic was the language used by Jesus and his disciples.***[6]

I also had the opportunity of checking the **HEBREW** word for **SPIRIT** in **H.W.F. GESENIUS'S** classical work, the **GESENIUS HEBREW-CHALDEE LEXICON TO THE OLD TESTAMENT.** The HEBREW word for SPIRIT is the word **RUACH.** I discovered from **H.W.F. GESENIUS'S** treatise, that RUACH is also **FEMININE.**[7]

These last set of facts confirm absolutely that the Holy Spirit is indeed the symbol of MOTHERHOOD.

AN IMPORTANT BALANCE

Now this does not mean we should now start saying ...**when "SHE" the SPIRIT IS COME!** NO...

This book is not about changing the gender of the Holy Spirit! The Holy Spirit is neither a MAN nor a WOMAN. This revelation about the Holy Spirit is an eye-opener into the tremendous ABILITIES that He possesses.

CHAPTER 8
SO WHAT

Let your imagination roam... imagine you gave this particular book on the Holy Spirit to a friend of yours. He reads from the first chapter right up to the seventh chapter. When he concludes the seventh chapter, his male ego is a little bruised... his defenses are up... he is looking for loopholes, so he can say... **"we men are not inferior"**. He puts the book down, raises one eyebrow, throws up both hands in exasperation and burst out...

"Okay so the Holy Spirit is the symbol of Motherhood, yes, SO WHAT?"

Thank God a man wrote this book. As I wrote earlier in the first chapter, this book is for both MEN and WOMEN. The Holy Spirit lives in both Men and Women. The issue of

MOTHERHOOD concerns us all.

The Holy Spirit is the **POWER** of the Trinity. Things are done **"THROUGH"** HIM or **"BY"** Him. Take a careful look at the following scriptures, make sure you read each one patiently:

> *Until the day in which he was taken up, After that he* **THROUGH** *the* **HOLY GHOST** *had given commandments unto the apostles whom he had chosen:* **(Acts. 1v2)**

> *And finding disciples, we tarried there seven days: who said to Paul* **THROUGH** *the* **SPIRIT,** *that he should not go up to Jerusalem.* **(Acts. 21v4)**

> *Through mighty signs and wonders,* **BY** *the Power of the* **SPIRIT OF GOD;** *so that from Jerusalem, and round about unto Illyricum, I have fully preached the gospel of Christ.* **(Romans. 15v19)**

> *How much more shall the blood of Christ, who* **THROUGH** *the*

*ETERNAL SPIRIT offered himself
without spot to God, purge your
conscience from dead works to serve the
living God?* **(Hebrews. 9v14)**

and finally...

*Then he answered and spake unto me,
saying, this is the word of the Lord unto
Zerubbabel, saying, Not by might, nor
by Power, but* **BY** *my* **SPIRIT,** *saith
the LORD of Hosts.* **(Zechariah.
4v6)**

Take careful notice of the words
"**THROUGH**" and "**BY**" in various scriptures
that have been given **above**. God does things
THROUGH the power of the Holy Spirit. We
cannot **ignore** the Spirit.

The comparison between the **"Holy Spirit"**
and a **"woman"** gives us a clear picture, an
insight into the workings and abilities of the
Holy Spirit.

JUST ALIKE

In the same manner that a woman is able to
GIVE BIRTH to a baby, the Holy Spirit has the

ability to **HELP** you **GIVE BIRTH** to the
MIRACLE or NEED you are believing God for!
It is His job to **HELP** you. Your "ANSWER"
comes **FROM** God, **THROUGH** the Holy
Spirit! When the Holy Spirit of God is absent,
there is a **missing link.** He is the bridge between
the other members of the Trinity and you.

SOMETHING HAPPENED

When I began to walk with the Holy Spirit my
life changed. As a minister of the Gospel, my
ministry changed. There came a point in my life
when I was asked the secret to the overflow of
the manifestation of the Spirit in my life! My
answer is... "it's my relationship with the Holy
Spirit". I need Him. I'm useless without Him.
I'm a failure without Him. I know what I'm
talking about! Over and over again, I walk up
and down my bedroom **TALKING** to the
mighty Holy Spirit, **FELLOWSHIPPING** with
Him. He is my best friend. Why don't you start
today? After you have finished praying to the
Father, ask the Holy Spirit to **HELP** you to
RECEIVE what you have prayed about. It is His
job: He is the **HELPER.** It is one thing for God to

GIVE you a "GIFT", it's another thing for you to **RECEIVE IT.**

RECEIVING

In the ministry of God committed into my hands, one day Holy Spirit started manifesting in services in tremendous **healing power.** I have lost count of the people that have been healed by the Lord without the touch of a human hand. The Lord has made it clear to me that it is not "my touch" but "His touch" that matters.

In service after service, I have done one particular thing over and over... I have asked the Holy Spirit to **HELP** people to **RECEIVE** their HEALING.

... It's by the SPIRIT

There have been times when I was amazed at the number of people who had been healed in a single service

...*It's by the SPIRIT*

> *But if the Spirit of him that raised up Jesus from the dead dwell in you, he that raised up Christ from the dead shall also **QUICKEN** your mortal*

> bodies **BY HIS SPIRIT** *that dwelleth*
> *in you.* **(Romans. 8v11)**

The word ´QUICKEN' in the passage above is the Greek word **ZOOPOIEO**, which means, **MAKE ALIVE.**

God will 'MAKE ALIVE' your sick body, your failing organs, your battered business, **THROUGH** the power and ministry of the Holy Spirit. Do you remember Simeon in the gospel of **Luke, Chapter two?**

> *He was a man that was told by God,*
> *that he would not die until he had seen*
> *JESUS* **(Luke.2V26).**

> *And it was revealed unto him by the*
> *Holy Ghost, that he should not see*
> *death, before he had seen the Lords*
> *Christ.* **(Luke.2V26).**

Simeon was given a **promise,** or we could go ahead and say he was given a **prophetic word** by the Lord, concerning his future.

Before this "WORD" from the Lord was given to him, we discover that he had a personal **RELATIONSHIP** with the Holy Spirit. It was after the development of this relationship with the Spirit that this tremendous promise about his future was released.

The latter part of **Luke. 2v25** declares:

> *... and the same man was just and devout, waiting for the consolation of Israel: and the* **HOLY GHOST WAS UPON HIM.** **(Luke 2v25b)**

Have you been in a situation where God has given you a strong **prophetic word** about a situation, but in the natural, you don't know how in the world it is ever going to come to pass? Circumstances seem so contrary to the word God gave! Time doesn't seem to be on your side! Let's enter into the arena of the imagination for while. Let's imagine what things were like for Simeon... or may I call him... Pa Simeon.

...The old man clutched his walking stick tightly, as he walked along the dusty road. A fresh gust of wind sent tremors through his octogenarian limbs. And though his joints were wracked with pain from age and fatigue, there was still a twinkle in those aged eyes, an unusual smile on that wrinkled face. Each step of his was slow and measured. There seemed to be

a hint of nobility locked up in the ancient frame... he walked with certainty, with purpose. Suddenly, a sharp blinding pain seared through his heart. Simeon stumbled forward, clutching and clawing at his chest. His gold – handle walking stick lay forgotten, as he sank to his knees gasping violently for breath. After what seemed to be an eternity, the pain passed, the gasping ceased. A few passers – by helped him to his feet. The twinkle was back in his eyes. The smile was back on his face. The old one continued his mysterious journey. He reflected on what had happened some moments ago. This had been his third heart attack in one week. The end seemed near, the hour looked close. But even though time seemed to be running out for old Simeon, he refused to let go of the PROMISE God made to him...

"Yaweh cannot lie", he said,

"He told me I would not die until I had seen the Messiah".

Simeon walked on into the glowing sunset, strangely warmed by a confidence in a God who could not lie...

One day his perseverance paid off. And truly as God had promised, it came to pass.

*And he came **BY** the **SPIRIT** into the temple: and when the parents brought in the child Jesus, to do for him after the custom of the law, then took he him up in his arms, and blessed God, and said, Lord, now lettest thou thy servant depart in peace, **ACCORDING TO THY WORD:** For mine eyes have seen thy salvation. (Luke 2v27-30)*

Eventually, the **promise** God gave to Simeon came to pass! But **HOW** did it come to pass?

You see, Simeon was **LED** by the Holy Spirit into the very temple where he would see the Messiah. If Simeon had not been sensitive to the instructions of the Spirit, he would have **missed** seeing the **promise** God gave him fulfilled.

Child of God, when all is said and done, we will still come to the reality that...It is by the Spirit.

CHAPTER 9
LAST WORDS

I once heard a story about an old American President... **Abraham Lincoln.** As the story goes, he used to find comfort in a mid-week service of the New York Presbyterian Church, during the height of the civil war. He would enter into the church with his aide, without causing any commotion among the congregation, and sit in the wings of the church. It proved to be a wonderful time of relief and release for him.

One day he sat quietly in a particular mid-week service, and as the service ended, he continued to sit, as the congregation left without even knowing he was there at the side. His aide leaned over and said to him.... *"what did you think of the sermon?"*. Abraham Lincoln replied that he thought the sermon was, *"well thought through"*, *"powerfully delivered"*, and *"very eloquent"*. But then he added... **"BUT IT FAILED"**. He went on... *"IT FAILED* because the Pastor did not *ASK SOMETHING GREAT OF US"*. In other words, he meant the preacher that night, had not made a demand on them to do something GREAT or NOBLE.[8]

In the mind of this great American president, who will never be forgotten in the annals of human history for his GREAT and NOBLE role, in the abolishment of the slave trade in America, the preacher had failed that night. That night men were not incensed, ignited to break through the mold of mediocrity into the green pastures of GREATNESS... "He asked nothing GREAT of us"!

Over and over again in the scriptures, we see the greatest preacher who ever lived, asking GREAT THINGS of the people that listened to Him. We see Him provoking people to leave the status quo and step into the mysterious milky way of GREATNESS. We see Him making fishermen into FISHERS OF MEN. We see Him turning death to Life, failure into victory, shame into glory. We hear His voice urging men into a new beginning. **"Go and sin no more".** We see Him asking something GREAT of Himself, when with hands outstretched, He gave His life on an old, rugged cross.

As you read this book, let me ask something GREAT of you! **Begin a very deep relationship with the Holy Spirit.** Don't take Him for granted. Don't ignore Him. He is a PERSON! He **talks, He feels, He cares.** When you call on Him, He moves in response to your cries. Please believe me, I KNOW HIM! Until you begin to walk with him, your life will be dry and powerless. Start today. A mighty relationship with the Holy Spirit, is just **few words away...** just a conversation away. Your journey with the Holy Spirit begins with **words.**

WITH THIS ROSE

Once, I was invited to speak at a church. The day before I was to speak, I had an unusual experience with the Holy Spirit.

I had decided to begin to treat the Holy Spirit like I would treat a person I loved and cared for.

I cut a rose from the rose garden that cool Monday evening, and went to the back of the house to commune with the Spirit. I lifted up the rose to the heavens and said "Darling Holy Spirit this is for you" ... then I told Him how much I loved Him, respected Him, appreciated Him... I went on talking to Him from the depths of my heart for some minutes, then I returned into the house.

I carried on my love speech to the Spirit even when I was in the house. Suddenly something unusual began happening... a sweet, sweet presence began wrapping itself around my being... oh! a sweetness beyond earthly description, beyond earthly vocabulary was claiming my being inch by inch... I could have lain down on the bare ground and worshipped God, just because of the "sweetness". With this sweet presence came a definite impartation of the Spirit.

The next day, at the church, the blessing I received the day before was let loose among the congregation and they rejoiced... I can't remember ever ministering under an anointing so "clean and crisp", so "sweet and life-transforming" – there was absolutely no strain or struggle, just a perfect "sweet purity" – an incredible force that pierced the very depths of the congregation.

I Left that church pulpit that day with a sense of awe upon my soul – Heaven seemed to be just round the corner. This particular experience with the Spirit, left an indelible mark upon my life... it created in me a hunger to walk even closer to the Spirit than I had been doing.

A CLOUD OF WITNESSES

A tremendous woman of God – **Kathryn Khulman** – A lady so mightily used of God in the miraculous had this to say...

> *"The secret of those bodies healed in the miracle services is the power of the* ***HOLY SPIRIT AND HIS POWER ALONE"***[9]

Pastor Benny Hinn, Pastor of the World healing Centre Church, in Texas, is a man known to millions as one of the great healing evangelists of our time. **Roberts Liardon** in his book *God's Generals,* writes the following about Kathryn Khulman and Benny Hinn:

"... It seems that Aimee Semple Mcpherson carried on where Etter left off, through great signs, wonders and exploits. I believe she received Maria's mantle. From Mcpherson, a similar mantle seemed to pass on to Kathryn Kuhlman. Kuhlman was also known for the great magnitude of miracles in her ministry and for her hunger for fellowship with the Holy Spirit. Today, in the 1990's, it seems to me that a similar healing mantle has passed from Kuhlman to Benny Hinn..."[10]

Pastor Benny Hinn has this to say about this early encounter with the Holy Spirit...

Since childhood I had heard about the Holy Spirit. He was part of the Trinity, and a member of the God head to be worshiped. Never had I thought of Him as a person to be addressed. What words should I use? Where should I start? I decided to begin the only way I knew – with my own simple vocabulary.

In my bedroom on Crossbow Crescent Street that night, I prayed, "Holy Spirit – Kathryn Kuhlman says You are her friend". I continued, "I don't think I know You. Now before today I thought I did. But after that meeting I realized I really don't". In child like faith I asked, "can I meet You? Can I really meet You?".

He continues...

There He was – the Holy Spirit had entered my room. And He was as real as the bed I was kneeling beside. For the next several hours I was crying and laughing at the same time. It was as though my bedroom had been lifted into heaven itself.

Again, he writes...

That experience in my bedroom was far beyond speaking in tongues... I was filled with His presence. For the first time, I met the person of the Holy Spirit. And from that moment forward He became my Counselor, my Companion, my Friend"[11]

Pastor Enoch Adejare Adeboye the *General Overseer* of **The Redeemed Christian Church of God,** whose headquarters is in Nigeria, West Africa, had this to say about the Holy Spirit...

*"I knew that if only I could become **closely associated** with the **Holy Ghost,** nothing could stand between me and what I wanted to do for God. Make the **Holy Ghost** your **friend** and the rest is easy.*

If you become the friend of the Holy Spirit, there is no limit to what God can do through you. If you begin to associate with Holy Spirit, those empty pews in your church will soon be overflowing with people.

You need the Holy Spirit more than anyone else, befriend him and every impossibility in your life will become possible.[12]

In **1998,** in what was dubbed **LEKKI '98,** the Lord use **Pastor Adeboye** to convene the largest gathering in the history of humanity. The **CNN** (Cable News Network) with an aerial satellite said the crowd present at a single service **could not be less** than **six and a half million people** (6.5 million). The next year, **1999,** in what was dubbed **FESTIVAL '99,** world was to witness a gathering of **thirteen million people** (13 million)"[13]

J. LEE GRADY the editor of one of the world's leading Christian magazines, *"Charisma and Christian Life"* confirmed this astounding African revival in his "First word" column of the **February 2002** edition of charisma:

He writes…

One of the most astounding spiritual awakenings in history is shaking Nigeria today. I saw it for myself in December, when I traveled to the city of Lagos to attend the **largest Christian gathering on the planet.**

He continues…

The numbers associated with this African revival are mind-blowing. On the second night of the Congress, I walked for 30 minutes into the crowd and never reached the back. A quarter of a mile further from where I stood, throngs of people were seated under a gigantic, pavilion-like structure with a metal roof that can seat an additional 1 million people.

I was told there were 10,000 ushers in the audience that night. They were stationed across a field that was wired with 2.5 kilometers of electrical cord for the sound system. Workers spent an entire year making the crude wooden benches that covered the dusty ground.[14]

The Pastor of one of the largest single congregations on the entire African continent - **Pastor Ray McCauley – Pastor of south Africa's Rhema Bible church** has this to say…

"The **Holy Ghost** *told me one time that I did not*

*treat Him **AS A PERSON.** Since then, there have been times I have turned my back on the congregation during a church service, and let the Holy Ghost completely take over, I have waited on Him. As a result, we've had sinners fall flat on their faces and not be released to get up until the altar call. Then they come forward and get born again".*[15]

Pastor Claudio Freidzon, an Argentinian Evangelist and Pastor with an International ministry, a man who for **seven years** had only **seven people** in his church congregation, writes:

*"I began to search God's face, to feed on Him. **I needed to know the Holy Spirit;** I needed His anointing. That was my real need! And when I sought him, he converted my wailing into a dance! He radically transformed my life and my ministry, leading me into paths never before imagined by me. After **seven years** of desert experience, I was led by a vision from God, to establish a prosperous church which today numbers over **4,000 members,** and he granted me the privilege of heading a revivalist ministry on a world-wide level".*

Again, he writes...

"Without a shadow of doubt, all virtue and capacity that others may see in me are exclusively the

*work of the **HOLY SPIRIT**, a result of my fellowship with him. I know that everything I have, I have through his grace, and that only he is worthy of all the glory.*[16]

Let me emphasize for a moment on a "line" that I quoted from Pastor Claudio's writings:

*... a result of my **fellowship** with him*

In the **thirteenth chapter** of Apostle Paul's second Epistle to the Corinthians, we are introduced to a dimension of spiritual activity called "FELLOWSHIP WITH THE SPIRIT".

*The grace of the Lord Jesus Christ, and the love of God, and the **COMMUNION** of the **HOLY GHOST**, be with you all. Amen.* **(2 Corinthians 13v14).**

The **Amplified Bible** puts it this way:

*The grace (favor and spiritual blessing) of the Lord Jesus Christ and the love of God and the **PRESENCE** and **FELLOWSHIP** (the communion and sharing together and participation) in the Holy Spirit be with you all. Amen (so be it).* **(2 Corinthians 13v14. AMP).**

The word **COMMUNION** that is used in the King James rendering of the above scripture **(2 Corinthians 13 v 14),** is the Greek word **KOINONIA.** This Greek word **KOINONIA** is translated into **different** English words in various parts of the Bible.

In **Hebrews 13 v 16,** it is translated as **COMMUNICATE.**

In **ACT 2 V 42,** it is translated as **FELLOWSHIP.**

In **Romans 15 v 26,** it is translated as **CONTRIBUTION.**

In **2 Corinthians. 9 v 13,** it is translated as **DISTRIBUTION.**

So, we can see that the word KOINONIA is rich with a variety of meanings. When we bring these various translations of the same word together, we get a more complete picture of what the Lord desired for His church. Through the **writings** of the **wonderful** Apostle Paul, the heart cry of God for the body of Christ comes ringing out... what is that heart cry? Amongst other things, it is the **COMMUNION** (KOINONIA) of the **HOLY SPIRIT** with the **BORN-AGAIN CHRISTIAN.**

Over and over again I find myself being invited to various congregations to speak about the **HOLY SPIRIT.** In one church I taught on the HOLY SPIRIT for around **fourteen weeks** consecutively.

Some of the greatest healings and moves of God I have experienced, have occurred when I preached in various churches about the HOLY SPIRIT.

When I look back at various lives that God has *affected* through the ministry he committed into my hands, I realize that one of the greatest things I did for those people was to tell them about the HOLY SPIRIT. When a person meets the Spirit and develops a *relationship* with Him, the Spirit will do the rest. As I have been writing line after line, I have felt the awesome anointing of the Holy Spirit coming upon me repeatedly.

Get ready… something incredible is going to burst loose in your life as you act upon what you have read in this book. As you begin a deep, real fellowship with the **eternal Spirit,** expect a visitation from God.

The best is yet to come.

REFERENCES

1. Finis Jennings Dake, *Dake's Annotated Reference Bible*, (Lawrenceville, Georgia: Dake Bible Sales, Inc., 1992), 280, 2nd and 3rd column.

2. James H. Strong, *Strong's Exhaustive Concordance*, (Grand Rapids, Michigan: Baker Book House Company, 1992), 12

3. W. E. Vine, *Vines Expository Dictionary of Old and New Testament Words*, (Tarrytown, New York: Fleming H. Revell Company 1981), 64.

4. International Learning Systems Corporation Ltd, *Chambers Encyclopedia* (New Revised Edition), (U. K: Hazell Watson and viney Ltd, 1970) 528.

5. Groiler Incorporated, *The American peoples Encyclopedia*, (New York: Spencer Press, Inc., 1948-1961), 2-245, 3rd paragraph.

6.   Cambridge University Press, *The Cambridge Paper back Encyclopedia,* (U.K:Cambridge University Press,1999), 43.

7.   H.W.F. Gesenius, *Gesenius' Hebrew Chaldee Lexicon to the Old Testament,* (Grand Rapids, Michigan: Baker Book House Company, 1979), 760

8.   Tape Series by Charles R. Swindoll, *Ministry Essentials,* Insight for Living, P.O. Box 69000, Anaheim, California 92817-0900, 1994

9.   Kathyrn Khulman with Jamie Buckingham, *A Glimpse Into Glory,* (Gainesville, Florida: Bridge – Logos Publishers, 1983), 111

10.   Roberts Liardon, *God's Generals Why They Succeeded and Why Some Failed,* (Tulsa, Oklahoma: Albury Publishing, 1999), 74

11.   Benny Hinn, *He Touched Me,* (Nashville, Tennessee: Thomas Nelson, Inc., 1999), 76 ,77.

12.   Tape by Pastor E.A. Adeboye, *My Closest Friend (the Holy Spirit),* Word & Sound Ministry, R.C.C.G. City of David, 23, Jimoh Odutolast, Iganmu, Lagos Tel:01-5850220

13.   Tony Ojo, *Let Somebody Shout Halleluyah,* (Surulere, Lagos: Honeycombs Cards and

Prints, 2001), 31

14. Strang Communications Company, *Charisma & Christian Life*, (Palm Coast, Florid: Strang Communications Company, 2002), 6

15. Rhema Bible Church, *The word of Faith, 10th Annual Camp meeting Special Edition*, October, (Tulsa, Oklahoma: Rhema Bible Church, 1982), 6

16. Claudio Freidzon, *Holy Spirit I Am Hungry for You*, (Sussex, England: Kingsway Publications, 1996), 40